LEADERS BREED LEADERS

The Seven Keys To Leadership

Leaders
Breed
Leaders

****

Copyright © 2010 by
Cedric Dean
****

****

BDB Publishing, LLC books may be purchased for educational, business, or sales promotional use. For information, please email: bbaker@ccdricdean.com

****
ISBN:978-1449591694
****

www.cedricdean.com

****

Contact Cedric Dean:
cedricdean@hotmail.com

This book I dedicate to the 9to 15 million at-risk
Youth who are traveling wrong. I pray that it will
Help bring them out of the dark to the light.

www.AboutSave.org

Acknowledgements

This year, two thousand and eleven, marks my sixteenth consecutive year of incarceration. I'm grateful to have some very loyal family members and friends who have been with me every step of the way. Through the trial, the appeals, the heartaches, the pain, and the rejections -1 was never alone. I've been blessed beyond measure. Words cannot express how my faith, family and friends have sustained me.

I'd love to mention them all by name, but there simply isn't enough page space. So to all those persons who have always loved, believed, prayed, enlightened, encouraged, empowered and cared for me - I appreciate and acknowledge YOU.

Lastly, to my fans that have supported me over the last couple of years, if I had a thousand tongues I couldn't thank you enough. May God Bless All Of You.

Cedric Dean

CONTENTS

Cedric Lamonte Dean

I was born June 14, 1972, in Charlotte, N.C. Betty Ann Dean, my mother, was only 18 and determined to raise me to be successful in life. After my birth, Mama and I lived in the projects. Billy Williams, the 19 year-old, who'd fathered me, came around to see Mama, hoping to repair their relationship. They had several rendezvous, and, to some extent, they continued to be attracted to each other. But Billy was a player, and Mama didn't enjoy being played, so she went her way, and he went his.

Growing up I always wanted a father, someone to take me out and spend time with me. I wanted to do all the things that I saw my friends doing with their fathers - playing sports, fishing, just hanging out and having fun.

Back when I was growing up there was a lack of parental development and a lack of focus. Being a single parent my mother was forced to work two jobs just to make ends meet, which meant that I was left at home with a lot of free time on my hands. Too much free time. In addition to her working at the City of Charlotte Water Department and cleaning office buildings, she was the church secretary. That left very little time for her to raise me. She was always busy with church things. For a long time I had the attitude that she really didn't care about anything that I was interested in. The only thing that mattered to her was serving God and providing for her son. I was really too young to understand. And so was she. She really didn't know what to do to save me from the streets. The reason she didn't know was because she unaware of who I was becoming and who I was hanging around.

In the fall of 1985 when I was 13-years-old, I was rebirth into a new world. The former youth choir member and Boy Scout was shown a brand new way of life. Being that my father wasn't the source of the love, guidance, and protection I sought, I began to search for those basic needs in the streets.

To demonstrate the gangster love I received in the streets, here is a rundown of how I was baptized into thuggery. I was introduced to an 18-year old ghetto superstar by the name of Timbo. He was a ganster's gangster and knew how to show gangster love. My best friend at the time, Marcus Massey, who was 14-years-old, introduced me to Timbo.

"It's good to see two young niggas who willing to learn the game," Timbo said in his thuggish terminology. "I can see you niggas have things you trying to get - shit your mama and daddy can't get for you. See, I know you wanna be sporting Jordon's and looking pretty for the hoes. But that shit ain't gon' happen unless you make it happen. If you trying to get paid, then you can - all you gotta do is let a nigga like me teach you the game."

Timbo did just that. He taught me how to be a gangster. He taught me how to get money, power and respect all at the same time. He taught me that a gun could help me get everything that I needed. See, kids believe what they see, and I saw clearly that Timbo was able to solve all of the problems he had with a gun. If he wanted some money, he'd rob a drug-dealer. If he wanted some respect, he'd shoot somebody for the fun of it. It fascinated Marcus and me to say the least. When we were with Timbo, we received the royal treatment. People went out of their way to look out for us. We got whatever we wanted - whenever we wanted.

Looking back, I'd say I carried a gun for three primary reasons. First - *for protection*. For example: In Charlotte there were a major problem with criminals robbing kids for their clothing, jewelry and money. Not to mention the upsurge in

7

gangs and violence. Living under these conditions created a climate of fear - and guns helped eliminate that fear. Second - *to commit crimes.* In my case I robbed drug dealers. Quite naturally that indirectly created violence because many of my victims tried to retaliate. And some were successful in shooting and killing many of my former acquaintances. Lastly - *to instill fear in others.* I wanted people to fear me as much as they feared God.

Today, many kids carry guns because they are paid to do so. A convicted felon like me is looking at a mandatory 5 years for carrying a gun, and 10 years or more for carrying a gun in relation to a crime. A child will get sent to training school and gain more street credibility.

In the 1990s more children were killed by guns than all natural diseases combined. There were simply more opportunities in the streets than there were in stores. In places like Chicago where 373 people were killed by guns in 2009, (highest per capita in the U.S.) there were a 25% unemployment rate among teenagers -50% among black teenagers. Kids with nothing to do feel that they have nothing to lose.

I'm often asked: "What is the solution to juvenile crime, drugs and violence?" I believe it's going to take *reason, restraint* and *resolve.* Without either one of them, our children are destined to fail. Timbo recruited me because he wanted to take full advantage of the fact that I wanted some big brother figures in my life. He used reason to get me to do some unreasonable things. And the right reason would've gotten me to stop. With restraint, kids don't have to be forced to do what's right. Restraint makes them do right for the right reasons. A pivotal part of teaching restraint is encouragement. Instead of telling kids what they can't do, we have to teach them what they can do.

Opposed to saying, "You can't sell drugs." Tell them, "You can sell cars. The principles are the same as the drug business — automobile dealers front people cars. They make commissions. They buy wholesale and resale at retail." Resolve deals with their decision making. I made more decisions in a day living the thug-life than the average adult. And 1 made most of them without thinking. And not thinking before I acted led to my demise.

In order for children to think before they act, they must see the adults around them doing it. I have an L - Plan: *Love, Labor* and *Leadership*. And it all starts with listening. If you listen you'll learn, then you can lead them into the right direction.

In 1984 when I embarked upon the thug-life, there were 34,000 juveniles serving Life Without Parole in the United States. (Source: *The Sentencing Project)* Today, there are over 140,000 juveniles serving Life Without Parole. Two-thirds are Black or Latino. The primary reasons for these horrific numbers are direct results from the following facts: 25% of American Students fail to graduate; 600,000 youth quit school in 2007-2008; (75% of state prisoners and 59% of federal prisoners are school dropouts) - School dropouts are 3.5 times more likely to be incarcerated. In 2008, juveniles accounted for 16% of all violent crime arrests. They were involved in 12% of all violent crimes. Eleven percent (1,740) of all murder victims was younger than age 18. More than one-third (38%) of all juvenile murder victims were younger than age 5.

None of us have the liberty of being apart from being human. Any child's death diminishes me because I am concerned about humanity. I have no despondency about the future - I have no trepidation about the outcome of my struggle to be free - even if my motives are often misunderstood. I will reach my goal of saving at-risk youth from premature death and incarceration because the goal of God Almighty is for all men, women and children to be saved.

In order to atone for my sins and errors while living the criminal lifestyle, I want to accept full responsibility of my actions and admit that I was wrong from the beginning of my criminality, and I acknowledge that my conduct was detrimental to the lives of innocent people in society.

So today I beg for forgiveness from every hard working American who must live in communities plagued with crime, drugs and violence. I am no longer affiliated with the criminal lifestyle, and I am profoundly apologetic that 1 once was.

There comes a time when doing nothing is selling out our children. When doing nothing is a direct breech of faith. When doing nothing is pulling a Judas. That time is now for us in relation to our children. The reality of these words is unquestionable but the duty to which they summon us is a very burdensome one. Even when forced by the orders of esoteric powers, we do not always easily accept the call to do what's morally right, especially when doing the right thing could create enemies from those engaged in doing wrong.

Over the past six years, as I have moved towards doing the right thing, many persons have questioned the sincerity of my transformation. At the heart of their concern these questions have frequently emerged vast and vociferous: "Why are you so eager to help the children? Aren't you a bad example for them?" And when I listen to them, though I usually understand the foundation of their concern, I am nonetheless deeply saddened, for such queries mean that the inquirers do not really know me, my dedication or my drive. Indeed, their questions suggest that they do not understand the circumstances that led to my downfall.

In the luminosity of such unfortunate false impressions, I regard it of great significance to attempt to say emphatically that my Christian faith calls for me to love my neighbor as I love myself. Specifically, Jesus said, "Whosoever shall receive one of such children in my name receives me." Contrary to popular belief, my life's experiences are a perfect example that there is always hope after making bad decisions.

Youth crime and violence must cease. Something must be done now. As a contribution to the solution, I have written this book and several others in hopes of reaching as many misguided minds as possible to inform them about the reality of the criminal lifestyle: death or incarceration.

I pray that you will find it in your heart to not only forgive me, but to work with me to help save our youth. I promise to spend the rest of my life securing a promising future for our children.

Yours for the cause of Love and Peace,

Cedric Dean

Foreword

Building community leaders out of public menace is the purpose of this curriculum. The principles of overcoming self-defeating behavior are outlined in simplistic terms for instruction by novice teachers, trainers and tutors. No matter if you are educating gangsters or gang bangers, addicts or adolescents, the moralistic precepts of leadership are the same.

The greatest way to change the world is to change the mindset of its misled people. They may have different ideas, different personalities and perspectives, but they all have a potential to change. And you have an opportunity to inspire and motivate them, just as the drug dealers and thugs who have led them astray.

An important thing to remember as you teach this course is not only the fact that change is possible, but the fact that the person who constructed this course is living proof of reform. In other words, a reformed criminal is teaching you how to reform criminal minded individuals. Yes, I am a living testimony. I've been to hell and back, and I know the secret to changing devils: compatibility. Misguided people have to identify with you before they'll consider what you're saying, and they aren't likely to heed if you do not understand them enough to relate to their experiences and encounters. Sometimes we miss out on the Don Kings and Charles Duttons, who served time for violent crimes but still, succeeded - we merely write them off and assume they're beyond rectification. The reality, however, is that until you really connect with an individual - sincere person to sincere person - making them see the light will be a more difficult task than it should be. People learn the most from people who understand them the most.

My desire for you is to catch the Martin Luther King Jr. spirit - *"whatever affects one directly, affects us all indirectly"* — and motivate and guide others to maintain a sense of dignity, self-respect and respect for others. You can lead by example in a way that is positively infectious.

As I look into the future, I see your leadership serving as a catalyst for others to start striving for excellence in all that they do. This course will help you help the misguided find their way.

INTRODUCTION A REALISTIC
IDEAL LEADERSHIP

Yes We Can - President Barack Obama

When I was growing up in Charlotte, N.C., the streets were at the center of my world. My spirits rose roaming around the drug-infested neighborhoods and seeing the dealers I idolized showcasing their Benzes and Beamers. I loved watching them shower the streets with their drugs, I loved helping them, and 1 would do anything to make them happy.

These ghetto superstars taught juvenile delinquents, like me, how to be the best gangsters they could be. They demanded the very best of me at all times, taught me the contrast between self-discipline and stupidity, and believed in me and helped me to believe in myself. They were not men of compromise; they would just as quickly put two bullets in your head as they would give every kid on the block an opportunity to make a $1000 a day. Yet they made the drug game an adventure and hustling a sheer delight.

One Friday night when I was 15, I was standing on the corner selling $20 bags of coke, and an addict tried to swindle me out of a bag, threatening to tell my mother that I was selling drugs if I didn't give him a free bag. As I thought about what my mother, who was a Christian, would do to me, I heard a voice from within say to me, "If you give him something this time, he'll expect something free every time he sees you." Before I could think twice about it, I removed a .38 revolver from my waistband and shot the man in the stomach. That was a mistake I've had to live with for over 20 years.

My mother found out two days later. I denied it to her, but I wore it as a badge of honor in the streets. I was just a fatherless kid who didn't know much about morality, but after seeing the tears in my mothers eyes as I eventually went to jail, I knew that I had hurt her more than the man who I'd shot. He survived, but, in prison, I was dead to the world. The way it starts is usually how it ends - at age 22, I received Life without parole for my involvement in a drug conspiracy.

Now that it's my turn to lead, I'm determined to teach the misguided how much of a mistake it is not to learn from my mistakes. What I have realized is much of what I learned from my negative influencers can be used positively and effectively. We've all seen the commercial on TV where the car driven by a dummy crashes into a wall. Well it's true, "You can learn a lot from a dummy."

I changed because many people refused to give up on me and write me off. Neither should you give up on the misled in your community. The single most important thing you can do is study the persuasive model of influence used by the gangsters and gang bangers who are brainwashing our children, and recognize how effective and relevant it is to saving our children - who are the future.

What are the criminals doing to convert children into cold-blooded creatures? They use the three (R)s: *recognition, regard* and *respect.* Converted into one (R) you get; *relationship.* Humans, in general, are inspired by relationships. Gang leaders listen to the wants and needs of their members. They listen to their problems without pushing them away. Everything matters to them all the way down to the slightest form of disrespect. Such little things make such a big difference. For instance: a member's sister may get abused verbally by her boyfriend. The gang leader will recognize the disrespect, regard it personally and respect the wishes of the member - even if it's an act of violence. Gang leaders display a genuine concern for their members, that's what compels the members to be at their beck and call.

Using a personal approach to leading bring forth genuineness and gratefulness. You'll get far more out of people by understanding them than you will by misunderstanding their circumstances and conditions. In this course I will discuss what 1 consider to be the top seven principles of effective leadership:

(1) Rapport

(2) Inspiration

(3) Drive

(4) Attitude

(5) Preparation

(6) Flexibility

(7) Integrity

These principles will help you improve others as well as yourself.

While teaching a GED class filled with prisoners, 1 learned that there's only one thing that stops a person from learning; *pride.* Or what Joanna Baillie dubs as, *"Pampered vanity,"* Something you can transform into promise.

After all, leadership is about performance not position.

RAPPORT
KEY-ONE

My leadership experience began at United States Penitentiary Coleman #1. It is a maximum security prison in central Florida, and I was very reluctant to be a leader. I accepted the responsibility of being the Executive Director of the facility's only inmate organization. I can remember the President, Lawrence Little, telling me, "It's time for you to use your influence over the inmates in a positive way. The same power that you once used to do wrong, you can now use it to get people to do what's right." I was in the process of writing, "How To Stop Your Children From Going To Prison," so I decided it would be hypocritical of me to say no.

When I started working with the younger prisoners, I could see right away that they were eager to participate in our many positive programs. That was my first challenge: getting them to adjust to the "No Profanity" rules for the program participants.

I gave them appropriate themes to perform to, and surprisingly, they didn't object. I recognized what mattered to them: attention. They simply wanted to appear on stage and be acknowledged for their unknown talents and abilities.

Having a good rapport with the prisoners allowed me to build a solid organization. But it all began by me having a legitimate reputation. When I tell one of the inmates, "this is what I am going to do for you," and then I do it, I earn their respect.

FIVE-KEYS

KEY-ONE: Communication

Communication is the middle ground between conflict and cooperation. Say what you mean, and mean what you say.

KEY-TWO: CONNECTION

Mohandas Gandhi once said, *"Character is mastery over your thoughts and actions."* In order to connect with anyone, a leader must have dignity, dexterity, dedication and diplomacy.

KEY-THREE: COMPASSION

People make mistakes. Past failures should never disqualify a person from future opportunities. Failures often make a person stronger and wiser.

KEY-FOUR: COURAGE

John Wayne illustrated courage as: *"Being scared to death - and saddling up anyway."* Leaders must be brave, bold and bullish.

KEY-FIVE: CHARISMA

Leaders are magnets that inspire others to follow their lead. They use the (3) Ps Power, Poise and Passion.

Discussion Questions

1) Who would you consider to be a great leader?

2) What prevents you from being a great leader?

3) What are you going to do to become a great leader?

Have your students to set (3) long-term leadership goals and (3) short-term objectives.

INSPIRATION
KEY-TWO

When I was transferred to United States Penitentiary Tucson, in Arizona, I was recruited to organize the prison's first intramural basketball league. Inmates do not like rules or structure, so I faced an immediate test.

I began by training the referees. I used the NCAA Official Rules Of Basketball as a training guide. To my surprise, the referees were enthusiastic.

I told them if they worked hard and strived for perfection, the players would respect their diligence. I made them practice decorum and discipline. It wasn't about policing the game; it was about professionalism. It was about providing a safe and satisfying league for the players.

When the season started, the inmates were stunned. The officials inspired the players to play like professionals. The most important lesson I taught myself that year was - proper preparation promotes professionalism.

There are many lessons to be learned from my tactics in dealing with problematic prisoners. First, there are ways to make points without making problems. When you set the precedent, you set the path of compliance. People have no problem doing what they see others doing - right or wrong.

The greatest leaders know how to get the best out of the worst among us.

FIVE-KEYS

KEY- ONE: SELF-CONTROL

Lead by example. Don't tell others not to do something if you're going to do it.

KEY - TWO: SELFLESS

People like to dream, but no one wants to be left out of the dream. Leaders don't consume happiness, they construct it.

KEY - THREE: SELF-CONFIDENCE

Samuel Johnson describes self-confidence as, *"The first requisite to great undertakings."* It is also the inner strength you can use to make others strong.

KEY- FOUR: SELF-ACCEPTANCE

You must be willing to admit when you're wrong and apologize when you wrong others.

KEY-FIVE: SELF-MADE

Leaders have the ability to lead because they have achieved success or prominence by their own efforts.

Discussion Questions

1) Who has been an inspiration to you?

2) Who have you inspired?

3) Who do you want to inspire?

Have your students choose (3) ways they are going to inspire others.

DRIVE
KEY – THREE

Recently, I was transferred to United States Penitentiary McCreary in Pine Knot, Kentucky. I was hired to doctor the ailing basketball league. I basically had more to lose than I had to gain by accepting the feat. The inmates were used to threatening the officials, and the referees had very little understanding of the rules to the game. To say the league was beyond repair is an understatement.

I prepared myself for the inevitable resistance. First, I was told by the outgoing overseers that I couldn't accept the job, because the league belonged to them. I had two options: stand up or lay down. And in prison when you lay down, you stay down.

I gave them an opportunity to look at themselves in the mirror by duplicating their aggression. In a composed manner, I told them, "I am a man and the league belongs to the men inside the prison." Afterward, I never heard another word about it.

Drive requires determination and demonstration. Once the officials and players heard about my stance, the stage was set for the show.

FIVE-KEYS

KEY-ONE: AMBITION

It's what Johann Goethe calls, *"The wings of great action."* It separates the boys from the men.

KEY - TWO: APPRECIATION

Leaders don't take anything for granted. They focus on the things they have control over and show gratitude to their helpers.

KEY - THREE: ACCURACY

Leaders never put more emphasis on one endeavor than they do another. They perform every task with proficiency.

KEY - FOUR: ARBITRARY

Leaders settle differences not start them.

KEY – FIVE: ARTISTRY

Henry James tags art as, *"The Shadow Of Humanity."* Leaders are creative craftsmen.

Discussion Questions

1) Do you strive for excellence?

2) Do you believe in shortcuts?

3) What are (3) of your shortcomings?

Have the students to come up with (3) ways to overcome their shortcomings.

ATTITUDE
KEY-FOUR

It is fair to say that being sentenced to Life Without Parole was the greatest challenge I've ever had to deal with. 1 remember seeing my family members lose control the day I was sentenced. I felt like I had failed them miserably.

For all practical purposes, my life was over, I was considered a dead man walking to the Federal Bureau of Prisons. There was only one problem. I never accepted that as being my fate. The period that the judge put on my sentence, I was determined to change it to a comma.

With the many accomplishments I've made over the last 14 plus years of incarceration, and the recent changes in the drug laws for cocaine base offenders, my positive attitude changed my destiny on September 16, 2009. My Life Sentence was reduced to 35 years. This means, I will not die in prison after all.

The foundation of maintaining a positive attitude is hope. It's the belief that the said end isn't the real end. In reality, this mindset saved my life. By taking proactive steps, I gave hope to my future.

In failure, a true leader knows it's not the end. He uses it as a highway to success.

FIVE-KEYS

KEY-ONE: FAITH

Edward Young eloquently describes faith in these words: *"A bridge across the gulf of death."* It's also confidence in your convictions.

KEY - TWO: FORTITUDE

It's that stick-to-itiveness that allows you to press on.

KEY-THREE: FORGIVENESS

Horace Bushnell terms it as, *"Man's deepest need and highest achievement."* It bears mentioning that Isaac Friedmann's meaning is quite uplifting: *"The sweetest revenge."* Leaders let bygones be bygones.

KEY-FOUR: FAIR

Leaders level the playing field. Every man deserves a fair shake.

KEY-FIVE: FUN

Fun is a planetary tie that ties all people together.

Discussion Questions

1) How is your attitude toward others?

2) How can you make it better?

3) How will you make it better?

Have the students name (3) ways to change a self-defeating mindset.

PREPARATION
KEY – FIVE

I've told many new prisoners who are awaiting an act of Congress to restore Federal Parole that if early release is renewed by lawmakers, there will be conditions. The board will expect clear evidence of a positive adjustment. Many inmates maintain clear conduct and assume that's substantiation of their rehabilitation. However, the verification must be more transformative. The board wants to see educational and vocational certificates. Employers need to see newly acquired skills. Good behavior is normal for law abiding citizens; it does not verify an ex-felon's ability to execute or hold a job.

The truth is that successful reentry always takes more planning than portraying, especially when it involves public safety. The high rate of recidivism is unmistakable confirmation of the small amount of time that goes into reentry planning. I tell prisoners every day that they should do at least one thing daily that better prepares them for society.

If you do the math that means a minimum of 365 deeds a year will go into planning their release. I wonder how many free men and women give half as much time shaping the things to come.

I mentioned what I encourage others to do daily; I didn't touch on the extent to which I go to planning for my own release. First, I start each day with a morning workout. By 8:00 am, I am teaching the first of (4) GED classes. During my lunch break, I usually tutor aspiring writers. From 5:00pm to 8:00 pm, I commission the basketball league. Afterwards, I wind down with some (me) time.

Productivity prescribes prosperity is a self-made affirmation I say again and again as a driving force.

KEY - ONE

KEY-ONE: OBEDIENCE

Focus on what needs to be done now; how you plan to attain success.

KEY - TWO: OBSERVATION

Examine your obstacles and devote attention to all philosophical changes needed.

KEY-THREE: OPTIMISM

A leader must be the ray of sunshine hidden behind the dark clouds.

KEY - FOUR: ORATORICAL

An Arabian proverb says an orator is *"One who can make men see with their ears."* Leaders are artful, articulate and artistic.

KEY – FIVE: ORGANIZATION

Leadership is about having your ducks in a row. Disorder disorients direction.

Discussion Questions

1) Where do you see yourself in five years?

2) What do you want to do to get there?

3) How are you going to do it?

Have the students list (3) long-term and (3) short-term set agendas.

FLEXIBILITY
KEY - SIX

While giving a lecture on essay writing, I was challenged by one of the GED students on the relevance of writing a perfect essay versus a passing one. The prisoner's exact words were, "I'm just trying to pass my GED. As long as they see I know how to write, I'll pass it. I don't care about using semi-colons and dashes — periods and commas work just fine for me."

I wanted to say, "well expect to get period and comma money for the rest of your life." Instead, I used a more tactful approach by asking the entire class, "If one of your children asks, "Daddy, what is the purpose of a semi-colon?" Who don't want to be able to answer the question?" No hands went up; not even my challenger's.

A leader has to be ready to bend at any moment. A mistaken notion of many leaders is that if they bend, it will show a sign of weakness. There is such thing as bending without breaking. While being resolute has its benefits, if a leader cannot adjust with the circumstances and contingencies of trials and tribulations, he will achieve only variable success because the real world rarely remains the same.

On the flipside, when a leader has a set agenda but remains open to change, he keeps himself ready for prosperity. In business, when the competition changes their prices, opponents began a battle royal. John Wright equates the jockeying for customers to, *"Riding a bicycle. Either you keep moving or fall down."* When an obstacle gets in your path, you must change your course.

FIVE - KEYS

KEY - ONE: RECOGNIZE

Acknowledge, analyze and absorb.

KEY-TWO: REASON

Apply logic by using your head.

KEY- THREE: REFERENCE

Seek advice, assistance and ammunition.

KEY- FOUR: REGROUP

Focus on one thing: what you need to do - or not do - in order to succeed.

KEY-FIVE: REMEDY

Counteract, correct and cure.

Discussion Questions

1) Name a time when you had to change your plans, but didn't.

2) What could you have done differently?

3) What will you do in the future to be ready for similar situations?

Have your class write an answer sheet for (3) potential future problems.

INTEGRITY
KEY - SEVEN

No man can be a real man without morals. Sigmund Freud once stated, *"Morality is feeling temptation but resisting it,"* I believe integrity is being able to say when you are wrong. I am not proud of who I was or what I did while living the street-life. I am proud of who I've become.

If you can't admit your faults, you cannot become a leader. Winston Churchill coined the cliché, *"Responsibility is the price of greatness."* I have done some destructive things to my community during my lifetime - things I look back and hate myself for. However, I've come to realize that the only way to stop doing wrong is by doing what's right.

George Eliot characterized regret as, *"The beginning of a new life."* Theodore Parker depicted remorse as, *"The pain of sin."* Somebody else said, *"Pain is the water for growth."* Here's what I have to say: Pain precedes positive pathways.

See, the potential is in the pain. It's not in the pleasure. It's not in the pandemonium. It's not always in the punishment. The potential is in the pain, and if you don't feel the pain, then you're paralyzed or psychotic. You have no integrity.

It's a grave mistake to ever quit. A quitter never wins and a leader never quits. With integrity, you can win at whatever you do and feel good about it.

FIVE - KEYS

KEY-ONE: EDUCATION

Education primes you to stand up against all temptations.

KEY-TWO: EFFORT

Effort is the sticker price to live on Easy Street.

KEY-THREE: EMPATHY

You must forgive to be forgiven.

KEY-FOUR: ENDURANCE

Endurance is the creator of good fortunate.

KEY - FIVE: EXPERIENCE

Oscar Wilde neologies experience as, *"The name everyone gives to their mistakes."* It is the source of a man's integrity.

Discussion Questions

1) What have your experiences taught you?

2) What have you learned from the experiences of others?

3) What can you teach others about your experiences?

Have the class think of (3) people they want to share their good/bad experiences with.

To the Teachers of America

My Most Honorable Teachers of America:

Growing up I wanted so bad to be a respected gangster, only to become one and realize that's not what I wanted to be. Gangsters don't live long. Gangsters retire to the penitentiary or the graveyard. And children should be shown this. Schools should maintain murals that list the names of children who are dead or incarcerated. In my book: How to Save Our Children from Crime, Drugs and Violence I conducted several interviews with prisoners. And among the questions were: "What should schools do to educate students about the consequences of violence?" A 26 year old Hispanic inmate by the name of Samuel Torrez said:

"School officials need to give more attention and more opportunities to kids who are poor and more likely to commit crimes. Teachers need to see which kids are on the right track and which ones are headed in the wrong direction. Too many teachers favor the jocks and not the kids who don't have the nice clothes and don't make the good grades. They need to take time to get to know who every kid is and find out about how the kid is living at home. If they try to get to know the kids' families personally, they'll be able to work as a team with the family to save the kids. The teacher can say in class, "Kids, I'm going to be meeting your families and spending time with you and them to get to know you on a more personal level, so I can help you be something in life." And the kids who try to stop the teacher from going to they're home will most likely be the ones who need the extra attention. At the end of the day, if you work at a school it shouldn't be just for money. It has to be out of love, too."

Additionally, I asked Samuel what school officials should do to deal with drug usage among students. His answer was:

"They really need to bring in real-life drug users - I'm talking about the bottom of the bunch. The ones with needle tracks in their arms. The ones with no teeth because they have been smoking too much meth. Those are the people they need to bring in to show the children who they will be looking like. My school could've offered more up to date activities. Instead of the major 4 sports - football, basketball, baseball and wrestling; the school should've offered mainstream music opposed to classical. I think they should've had better motivational speakers. Not the average person who has never experienced a damn thing in life but tries to teach us how to live. Instead of showing us a video of someone dying of AIDS - the school should've brought 4 or 5 dying AIDS patients to the school."

Moreover, I cannot sit idly in prison and not be concerned about what is happening to our children. School dropouts anywhere are a danger to communities everywhere. We must unite in a necessary network of support and sympathy, coupled by an upright guiding principle of love. Everything that concerns one child negatively, concerns all children in some way. In no way can we afford to give up on our children. To give up on them is to give up on the future of America.

Now is the time for you to care for each child as you care for your own. My hope and my desire is to see every student, every dropout every delinquent - every young person - aspire higher. My expectation is that your lessons will move and motivate them and give them the courage to reach for their dreams; and that the great minds you possess will become their own.

I was not supposed to become a teacher and transform gangsters into gentlemen inside of prisons, but I made a promise to the people who helped me along the way that I would help others who are living like I used to live. 1 didn't think it was possible for someone with a past like mine to be given the opportunity to teach anyone anything. But I was. And I feel good every single time one of my GED students get their diploma. I feel even better when I receive a letter from a person who I've had the pleasure to inspire write me from the free world with their success story. When you give back, God has a way of blessing you with so much more - you and others.

When I look back at the path of my own life in the streets and the gangsters who were around me, I see clearly that the path chosen for me was teaching. The thug-life was a big scam. The experiences it provided were unforgettable and it was certainly unfavorable, but I realize now that it was all preparing me to teach. My adolescent years robbing and drug dealing prepared me to deal with the youngsters who enter the Federal Bureau of Prisons with no sense of direction, and youngsters whose hope is all but gone. The good people I met on the way prepared me to learn how to deal with the misguided, and my misfortunes prepared me to teach others the mistake in not learning from my mistakes.

Now, I believe I can teach in any capacity. That's not an egotistical statement. I can teach gangsters, gangbangers, drug dealers and delinquents because I know what it's like to be them. It's my life's calling. Education comes from experience. Experience is the greatest teacher. It's an excellent school but the fees are costly. It's the name we all should give to our mistakes. Children must be taught that it's a mistake not to learn from our mistakes. That they don't have to travel the same roads that we've traveled just to learn the lessons we've learned.

The reality is this, if you know children who are living in a pessimistic, unsympathetic environment, you must teach them how to not allow it to shape their attitudes. Teach them not to allow their environment to destroy their destiny. Don't let it destroy their dreams. Convert the venom into virtue by thinking before they act. In a pessimistic environment, it's tough to not go with the flow. It's tough to say no when everyone else is saying yes. It's tough.

This is the time for you to teach them about them. It's time for you to help them see themselves as the world sees them. It's time to teach them that the people who they think are their friends really aren't. Everybody who pretends to love them really doesn't. You must convince them to limit the amount of time they are spending with people who are not where they want to be in life. You have to teach them the most powerful word in the English language - NO! It is the one word that can save them from crime, drugs and violence. Do you want to rob a bank? NO! Do you want to get high? NO! Do you want to kill someone? NO!

Most children feel that teachers need to try harder to relate to how it is to be a kid in this era. The quickest way for you to get shut out is by asking questions children feel are trick questions. Questions that children cannot answer honestly without being severely chastised. For a lot of inner city kids the number one issue for them is how they're going to get safely to and from school. In Chicago, getting to school is all about survival. If kids are non-affiliated to gangs they're bound to get picked on. How can they possibly concentrate on their grades if they don't even know if they're going to make it home safe from school?

Before you try to compel your children to aim higher, you must get them to get to know themselves. I did that early in my incarceration. I was questioned by model inmates who would ask me: Who are you? What do you want out of life? What is your purpose? They showed me that they cared about me and my future, so I began to care myself and ponder over those questions. I decided that I wanted to be a better person. I also wanted to have a positive impact on the lives of other misguided youth. Learning who I was helped me to learn what I wanted to do with my life.

Finally, and maybe most importantly, you must teach your children to believe in themselves. Believe that they have the willpower to accomplish anything in life. No matter how bad off they may be. For the success I've had it wasn't simply my writing skills that garnered it, it was the countless number of mistakes I made and the rejections I received along the way. They made me stronger, wiser and better.

Yours for the cause of Love and Peace,

Cedric Dean

Plea for Peace to School Kids

My young brothers and sisters:

I've been incarcerated altogether for more than 20 years of my life. I hope that this brief message will get you to think about your future and the future of America.

The crisis of criminal conduct and violence has stained the fabric of our great nation. It has divided families and destroyed communities. It is obvious today that America is doomed unless you begin to take life more seriously. You are the future of this nation and the future of this world. Without you, there is no future. Without your great minds there will be no new inventions or creations.

So I am asking you today to restore the future of America by restoring the values of America. Values are the standards that you should live by - beliefs, morals and laws. Now is the time to move from the dim and depressing desert of destruction to the sunny pathway of decency. Now is the time to unlock the gates of opportunity for all of America's youth. Now is the time to save our country from the villains of violence and the demons of death.

You must strive to be better than others expect you to be in order to be someone in this world. You must strive to exceed your own expectations in order to have the things that you want in life. If you cannot change when circumstances demand it, how can you expect your life to change for the better? The day I am afraid to change for the better is the day that I am no longer fit to live.

The hearts, souls and minds of each of you can rise. Power is not in violence. Power is in your ability to use mind. The more you think, the more powerful you become

Young men, there is a thing called respect. First, you must always respect yourself. You must always treat others the way you want to be treated. You should never disrespect women. Women delivered us into this world -without females males wouldn't exist. The next time you disrespect a female, think about how you would feel if someone disrespected your own mother. That's how others feel as well. Nowadays instead of doing things to please females, males are doing things to please other males. *This is for my dog!* A dog is an animal, and as long as you act like a dog you will get treated like an animal. And animals stay chained up and confined to one area.

In closing, I just want to know that your failure is America's failure. You can be whatever you will if you give yourself a chance. Always love yourself and everyone else. In God's eyes we're all the same. I cannot save you, but you can save yourselves.

Yours for the cause of Love and Peace,

Cedric Dean

(Diversify)

Society is clearly suffering, and because of where we are, our children are in dire need of guidance and a new direction. If you look at society, we must diversify ourselves as much as possible. We live in a world where our skills and trades distinguish who we are. I've seen huge amounts of talent within these walls. If only we knew how to channel it and harness it, we could seize anything we want in the whole world. It's our choice to do so.

Sometimes prison can be so stressful to me, but at other times I am half thankful for the life I've lived because it gives me the opportunity to look through life through the eyes of many individuals, and it gives me purpose and a new meaning to life. I'm not here to preach. I'm just here to encourage you to make use of your time. To encourage you to *do you* ~ To be the best *you* that *you* can be. To lead yourself in the direction that you want and need to go in. To get you to think about being responsible to *you and yours*. I took the HVAC class because it pays to have a trade - a foundation to stand on when we re-enter into society. To be able to support my child and family. I attended the first Leaders Breed Leaders workshop because Cedric Dean asked me to and because we are like chameleons...we quickly adapt and adjust to our habits and surroundings. And we need to surround ourselves around people that we want to be like. People like Cedric Dean, and Eugene Linwood - they are teaching classes and trying to better themselves and others. If we surround ourselves around positive people we will obviously become positive people. That's just food for thought.

No one is perfect. Not certainly I - or for that matter - nor any individual in this room - staff or inmate. We all have faults and flaws, but at the same time, we all have an equal opportunity to leam from our mistakes and take heed of what we need.

In closing, I want to say this - there are probably a lot of people in this room that would have thought that I would be the last person in this prison standing up here and saying what I've said - but you can never judge a book by its cover. You never know what's inside of it until you open it up and read it. I said that to say this, there are still many pages to be written in the chapters of our lives. I encourage you t be the writer - articulate your lives in positive ways and *do you!*

Thanks for your time and enjoy the rest of the seminar.

By Shannon Silknitter

Shannon is a 22 year-old federal prisoner who gave this speech at one of Cedric Dean's Leaders Breed Leaders Seminars at United States Penitentiary Lee in Jonesville, Virginia.

(Exclusive Interview)

Jeffrey Spurlock is a 28 year old native of Phenix City, Alabama who is serving 78 months for possession of a firearm. He is currently pursuing a career in cosmetology and he has high aspirations of working with at risk youth upon his release. Cedric sat down with Jeffery at United States Penitentiary Lee to discuss the state of America's children.

Cedric: How can America save its children from resorting to a life of crime?

Jeffery: The best way to help children is to make sure every child has a reliable provider who will be able to adequately care for the child, as well as make sure the child learns to go about the right way to having things.

Cedric: How old were you when you began committing crimes? And how were you influenced to start?

Jeffery: I was eleven. Another kid who was about 16 was breaking into houses and stealing CD players and jewelry. He didn't have anywhere to take the stuff so he brought it to my house, because my folks were cool. I would hold the stuff and he would give me certain things, but eventually his sister turned him in and he in turn brought the police to my house. That was how I got exposed to the criminal lifestyle.

Cedric: What could your community have offered to you that would have prevented you from being a criminal?

Jeffery: I would say the community needs to have more things for the children to do that are closer to their neighborhoods. I grew up in the country and I just ran wild, because there weren't any organized activities. As a result, it led me to hang out with older people who ended up having a negative influence on my life.

Cedric: What could your school have offered you that would have prevented you from being a criminal?

Jeffery: For kids who wanted to play football and other sports, a lot of people's folks couldn't afford to buy the stuff they needed to participate or afford to transport their kids back and forth. Afford or have time. Schools need to create programs that will either donate money or help raise money for underprivileged children.

Cedric: What could your parents have done differently to prevent you from becoming a criminal?

Jeffery: It wasn't anybody but my mom. She tried to do everything to raise me and my 2 brothers. We used to always be by ourselves because our mom was constantly working. We practically raised ourselves.

Cedric: What impact does drugs have on the criminal lifestyle?

Jeffery: I would say a big impact because a lot of people can't afford drugs and end up doing illegal
stuff to try to support their habit.

Cedric: What should the community do to combat drug usage among youth?

Jeffery: The community needs to show the kids that there are more ways to have fun than with drugs and more ways to make money. It starts out with kids smoking a little weed or drinking to have fun. Then they realize that you can make a lot of money off of drugs and get high. So the community needs to provide more ways for kids to have fun and make money.

Cedric: What should school officials do to deal with drug usage among students?

Jeffery: I think the uniforms are a good step in the right direction, because a lot of kids use drugs because they get depressed about not having the same things that everyone else has, such as clothes, shoes and jewelry - materialistic things. It makes the kids who don't have nice things feel bad. Everyone should appear equal at school.

Cedric: What should parents do to save their children from drugs?

Jeffery: Give them more activities to keep them busy and monitor where they go — know who they are with and where they are at all times. Some kids have too much free time. I had entirely too much free time.

Cedric: How can America save its children from violence?

Jeffery: The community needs to be more observant of kids and who they are around. A lot of kids join gangs for attention or protection. And that should come from the community, family and school.

Cedric: What should the community do to stop the violence among gangs?

Jeffery: The community should try to engage gang members with a meaningful channel of communication. And then try to fill whatever voids are in their lives. They are human beings and should never be given up on.

Cedric: What should parents tell their children about violence?

Jeffery: That violence is not the way - there are other ways to solving problems. Parents got to be a good influence on them. Teach them how to not put themselves in the situation in the first place to have to commit a violent act. Prevention is the key. Kids get put into situations and feel obligated to do something.

Cedric: What should schools do to educate students about the consequences of violence?

Jeffery: Schools need to teach kids how to be more positive towards each other. Most kids are too negative. Schools need to educate children about the penalties of crimes. Most children have no idea how much prison time they can get for various crimes.

Cedric: Thanks for everything that you said. And I wish you the best.

Jeffery: Thanks to you for giving me this opportunity. I just want to add one more thing — America needs to provide more jobs for everybody. You have parents who can't provide for their kids. We need more programs for kids to start learning trades at a younger age. Trades that they can get paid for as they learn. They need to see the value of hard work and money.

INCORPORATE YOUTH

How to involve youth in decision – making

Incorporate Teens

In order for juveniles to truly understand public justice, we must build a nation in which teenagers are complete citizens, given power to share thoughts and make decisions. Teen involvement is an initiative whose moment has arrived. Teens are often prohibited from making key decisions that affect teenagers, when in fact teens are the only ones who can truly represent the spirit and interests of teens. It's time for our nation to listen to young people. Young people do majority of the wrong things that they do to get attention - they want to be heard and they want to participate in decision-making processes that affect their lives and the communities in which they live in.

This section outlines effective ways to get youth involved in key decisions that affect them and their communities. It also offers ideas about how local, state and federal governments can successfully create a civilized and caring environment which youth can live together in love, peace and happiness.

It is important that we give our young people a chance to have a say into what direction their lives are to go in. One of the benefits of having young people involved in decision-making is that they insist on sincerity and reliability, on asking why certain decisions were made. They dare others to think imaginatively and think about new ways of doing old things

Advantages of incorporating youth in decision-making

For the nation

- ❖ Balances the representativeness of decision-making. Teens make up an important percentage of the nation. They also bring innovative thoughts and vibrant perspectives about the future.
- ❖ Helps the nation make better decisions. A balanced variety of views and experience can strengthen the decision-making process.
- ❖ Helps the nation improve its services for youth. Adults can serve youth better if they have a better understanding of them.
- ❖ Improves the image of America. Creating a youth-friendly America inspires the confidence of our children and enhances the reputation and credibility of the country.
- ❖ Help encourage youth to become volunteers. Incorporating youth as decision-makers indicates that America is serious about dealing with youth respectfully and encourages young people to assume an array of roles

For Youth

- ❖ Builds self-worth and self-confidence Taking on responsibilities for directing a community provides for leadership and is an important step in a young person's maturity.
- ❖ Develops significant skills, Leadership, decisive thinking, problem solving, consensus building and networking are among the skills that can grow out of participating in the decision-making process.

- ❖ Provides experience pertinent to education and employment. Undertaking decision-making roles enables young people to fulfill community involvement requirements for graduation while teaching skills that are not always learned in the classroom. It also helps young people plan their careers, build their life-skills and gain skills that will be valuable on the job.

- ❖ Gives youth an innovative and creative channel for their energy and creativity. Youth are sometimes stereotyped as being arrogant or lazy. The task that comes with decision-making will prove these stereotypes wrong. Inviting young decision makers to the table creates promise and opportunity for them to be appreciated for what they have to offer.
- ❖ Connects youth to other youth and to their community. Giving young people a stake in decision-making improves their understanding of residency and connection to other individuals and establishment within their community.

For Neighborhoods

❖ Neighborhoods gain from having youth participation because they bring bright ideas, new vision and new life. For your people, it's impossible to expand decision-making skills unless you are in that role and learning from those with the experience. Young people bring vigor, optimism, hopefulness and big picture thinking that can help any neighborhood.

❖ Overcome unconstructive stereotypes about youth and creates new respect for young people. It allows them to demonstrate their skills and commitment and put to rest the preconceptions and mistrust that often cloud the relationship between youth and adult society, It also builds inter-generational partnerships that do well to the entire community.

❖ Strengthens neighborhood power and neighborhood equality. Giving youth a stake in decision-making builds a broader base of resident involvement and creates stronger, more inclusive communities. Youth engagement also builds commitment to the whole range of teen groups that serve neighborhoods in so many different ways. Everyone profits when teen groups are successful and structured.

How to make youth decision-making a success

It is important to create a space where the younger generation is not just observers. Some of the things to think about in accomplishing this are the timing of meetings, so that youth can attend, how meetings are structured so that everyone has an chance to speak, giving youth proper orientation and opportunities for informal mentorships to grow with experienced community members. When involving young people you have to give more thought into what supports and additional training might be needed. It's also important to do informal check-ins after meetings to find out how they found the meeting and whether the youtli feel they were heard.

What you need to look at...

❖ Look at your community's guiding principles and practice on comprehensive decision-making. Does the decision-making in your community fully reflect your community? Discuss the value of inclusiveness and the value of having youth at the table. Youth are an important population group to consider but there may be others to consider as well.

❖ Be certain that the residents of your community are willing and able to collectively support youth participation. Youth involvement in decision-making will not work without the whole-hearted support of your community; particularly those who are lawmakers and government officials. They must be prepared to submit at least some of the rights of adult power.

❖ Build understanding about the value of listening to the voice of youth. Lay the foundation carefully to help all parts of your community understand the value of inviting young decision-makers to the table.

❖ Plan your approach. Establish a structure for youth engagement. Determine what kind of involvement makes the most sense for your community - policy development, program planning or evaluation - and how it can be matched with the particular skills and interests of the young people. Plan ahead for outreach, orientation, and training for volunteers and any other resources that may be needed. Review the existing communal culture and determine how it might create barriers for participation by youth.

❖ Be prepared to treat youth as equal participants in the decision-making process. Youth will quickly become aggravated and disaffected if they feel they are being patronized or denied equal status

Making Choices

❖ Be clear with youth participants about the expectations, responsibilities, scope of decision-making authority and other practical details of the role that you are inviting them to take on. Discussing expectations will ensure that the young person is prepared and well informed to make the right decision. The right fit is important and will ensure success for both the young person and the community. Communities need to consider their own needs and choices for success.

❖ Make diverse selections. Like all appointed positions, the selection of young people will be most beneficial if it representative - from ethno-cultural, class and geographic perspective - of the community they will serve.

❖ Ensure that young decision-makers are not isolated. Invite more than one young person to join the advisory board or committee to provide mutual support.

❖ If youth are elected or appointed as representatives, ensure that reporting and accountability mechanisms are clear. To get full value for youth participation, communities must have clear channels of communication and reporting to all involved members.

❖ Recognize and address legal and systemic barriers. Youth under the age of 18 may not be legally eligible to vote as members of the board but still may have important contributions to make to decision-making.

Getting Acquainted

❖ Create an environment that is welcoming to both physical and social terms. Ensure that the physical space in which you meet is not intimidating and that all adult participants are prepared to be friendly and accommodating to new decision-makers

❖ Provide orientation to the community. Ensure that residents understand what the community is trying to achieve

❖ Schedule meetings at a time that match the busy school and work lives of youth. Daytime meetings can create time conflicts that make it difficult for youth to participate effectively.

❖ Make sure the location is not a barrier to participation. Work out transportation needs, etc.

❖ Provide refreshments and snacks. Young people have larger appetites than adults do because they are growing and lead active lives. Providing cold beverages, snacks or a light meal, if the meeting time coincides with meal times, goes a long way to ensure their active participation.

Making it work

Adults need to understand what youth are all about. One idea is to have youth facilitate a training session, almost like a cultural studies workshop. Through this they can teach the adults what's cool and what's not, decode jargon and interpret behaviors to break down misunderstandings. Informal times like dinner before the meetings are good times for leaders and youth to interact get to know each other in a friendly environment.

❖ Match youth decision-makers with mentors from the community. Provide the time and opportunity for a relationship of trust to develop before youth are selected. The mentor should be available to provide information and answer questions that the young person has about the process, vocabulary and other issues as they arise.

❖ Provide ongoing training to help young people develop the skills they need to be effective decision-makers. Recognize that there is likely to be turnover in youth membership and that it may be necessary to replace youth decision makers more frequently than their adult counterparts. Young people are at a point in their lives that brings about change. They move from one school to another or they enter the employment field. Change is a significant factor that distinguishes youth from adults.

❖ Think outside of the box. To make it work, you may have to constantly remove barriers and to really keep an open mind. Some of the specific things a community can do to include young people are structure meeting that are politically incorrect, and accept young people as they are

61

❖ Recognize that the relative inexperience of youth can be both a strength and a weakness. Youth can bring fresh, new perspectives to the table, but need time to develop an understanding of a community's history and challenges. Create a respectful decision-making environment that balances those strengths and weaknesses.

Fifty Keys To Safeguard Your Future

TEN KEYS TO IDENTIFY INSINCERITY

1) When people are deceptive, they're likely to cover their mouth, eyes or ears while talking.

2) Shyster's use fake smiles, nods and winks.

3) Look for repetitious touching of the nose.

4) Deceivers usually rub their eyes vigorously.

5) Watch for five or more scratches with the index finger below the earlobe on the side of the neck.

6) Some people pull on their collars when they are deceitful.

7) Stuttering or word hang-ups are instant signs.

8) Lack of eye contact is another indicator.

9) Note echoing your questions or statements.

10) Watch for hands clenched together. (All body language gestures should be read in clusters of (3) constant movements.)

TEN KEYS TO MAKING THE PERFECT FIRST IMPRESSION

1) Never talk using your hands.

2) Use the person's name correctly.

3) Never talk for more than thirty seconds at a time.

4) Use powerful words.

5) Always maintain eye contact.

6) Mirror the other person's gestures and expressions when appropriate.

7) Always be on time.

8) Don't accept phone calls during meetings.

9) Dress appropriately.

10) Never say, "You know what I'm saying."

TEN KEYS TO AVOID PROBLEMS

1) Never promise to do more than you're able to.

2) Always know what you're being asked to do.

3) Don't spread rumors.

4) Don't intimidate others.

5) Don't mislead people.

6) Make your own decisions.

7) Be careful what you accept from others.

8) Never lend more than you can afford to lose.

9) Never borrow more than you can afford to pay back.

10) Just say, "No!" It'll save you a lot of trouble.

TEN KEYS TO HIRING SUCCESSFUL PEOPLE

1) Be clear about who you are and what you stand for.

2) Share a personal experience.

3) Share your vision.

4) Make the person feel comfortable.

5) Ask for their idea of honesty.

6) See what their short and long-term goals are.

7) Never use pressure.

8) Inquire about past failures.

9) Discern those who've learned from their mistakes from those who haven't.

10) Always remember, "Eyes don't lie."

TEN KEYS TO SOLVING PROBLEMS

1) Gather the facts.

2) Assess the facts.

3) Evaluate the consequences.

4) Use sound judgment.

5) Exert courage to act.

6) Act in a timely manner.

7) Act appropriately.

8) Avoid making new problems in the process.

9) Be able to live with your resolution.

10) Be sure others can live with your remedy.

FIFTY SECRETS YOU CAN SHARE

TEN SECRETS TO TRANSFORMATION

1) Stay away from negative people.

2) Admit your faults.

3) Ask for help.

4) Always be positive.

5) Write down specific goals and how you want to reach them.

6) Don't let what others think distract you.

7) Acquire new skills.

8) Keep it simple.

9) Always be honest with yourself.

10) Never give up.

TEN SECRETS TO SUCCESS

1) Think about the opportunities, not the obstacles.

2) Make reasonable, rewarding and retrievable goals.

3) Don't be afraid to make mistakes.

4) Work hard.

5) Be willing to learn from others.

6) Never waste time.

7) Be unique.

8) Network.

9) Don't cheat yourself or others.

10) Be responsible.

TEN SECRETS TO A SUCCESSFUL MEETING

1) Set the agenda.

2) Allot a specific time to discuss each matter.

3) Keep good notes.

4) Be the last one to speak.

5) Ask questions before making any decision.

6) Evaluate the other point-of-views.

7) Play Devils Advocate.

8) Share your thoughts.

9) Evaluate strengths, weaknesses, opportunities and threats.

10) Make a decision that's in everyone's interest.

TEN SECRETS TO CREATIVE WRITING

1) Be original.

2) Write an outline of your ideas.

3) Know what you want your readers to think, feel and wonder.

4) Present a clearly focused main idea.

5) Always use specific and relevant details and examples.

6) Use a varied and precise word choice.

7) Make every word count.

8) Always state your positive intent first.

9) Never write anything you wouldn't want to read.

10) Write safe, satisfactory and soulful.

TEN SECRETS TO EFFECTIVE COMMUNICATION

1) Listen to comprehend.

2) Speak to be understood.

3) Say what you mean.

4) Mean what you say.

5) Never assume.

6) Ask clarifications questions (Who, What, When, Where

   and Why)

7) Always be respectful.

8) Speak only about what you know.

9) Think before you speak.

10) Agree to disagree when you don't agree.

Afterword

The principles that I've outlined are universal and can be used in any setting. They've helped me to redirect some of the country's most notorious criminals to positive and productive paths. Sure, there is a stark difference between criminals and citizens. But contrary to popular belief, criminals are also human beings. And all human beings have the potential to change. Some just don't want to. Regardless of that misfortunate, I've found that all humans are moved in much the same way.

The best followers make the greatest leaders, mainly, because they are determined not to make the same mistakes of their predecessors. Time can change anyone. It's a natural fertilizer. It's soul food. Every plantation needs a good farmer - a planter, cultivator and sharecropper. Farming is about crop-raising, harvesting and working the land. Thomas Jefferson called it, *"The first and most precious of all the arts."* Matching his eloquence, Emile C. Alain called it, *"A school of patience: you can't hurry the crops or make an ox in two days,"* Go work the land and see how many leaders you can raise. The soil I've given you is very fertile.

LEADERS BREED LEADERS

About the Author

CEDRIC DEAN is a leader, an educator, and occasionally even a psychologist, but for the most part, he is a mentor, motivating the misguided with the same sizzling enthusiasm that allowed him to transform from a gangster to a genius. Growing up in Charlotte, N.C., he had aspirations of being a thug, but after regimented years of learning, labor and loneliness, he persevered. Cedric's personal and prison experiences shed light on critical lessons and have roused correctional staff and inmates at his *Leaders Breed Leaders* seminars. His transformational message has touched the lives of countless misguided individuals across the nation.

For more information about Cedric Dean,
please visit www.cedricdean.com .

To order, visit www.cedricdean.com or photocopy the form below and send to:

BDB Publishing, LLC
P.O. Box 30832
Charlotte, N.C. 28230

Send me _____ copies of

Leaders Breed Leaders

$8.95 + 2.95 for USPS Shipping and Handling

Please Print

Name _____

Address _____

City _____ State _____ Zip _____

My check or money order is enclosed.
Please make checks payable to BDB Publishing, LLC.

For other exciting books by Cedric Dean
please visit:

www.cedricdean.com